CHICKEN SOUP
WITH RICE

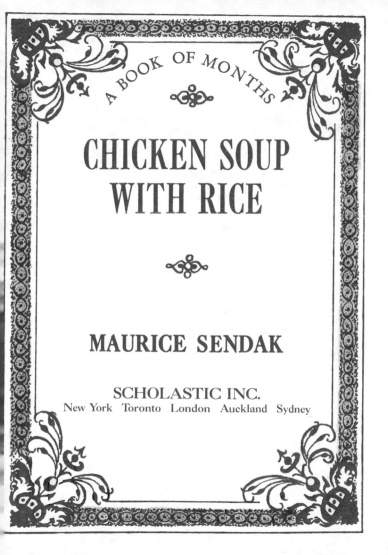

A BOOK OF MONTHS

CHICKEN SOUP WITH RICE

MAURICE SENDAK

SCHOLASTIC INC.

New York Toronto London Auckland Sydney

ISBN 0-590-45452-8

Copyright © 1962 by Maurice Sendak.
All rights reserved. Published by Scholastic Inc.,
730 Broadway, New York, NY 10003, by arrangement
with HarperCollins, Publishers.

20 19 18   8 9/9 0 1 2/0

Printed in the U.S.A.   08

First Scholastic printing, January 1992

For
Mrs. Ida Perles

JANUARY

In January
it's so nice
while slipping
on the sliding ice
to sip hot chicken soup
with rice.
Sipping once
sipping twice
sipping chicken soup
with rice.

FEBRUARY

In February
it will be
my snowman's
anniversary
with cake for him
and soup for me!
Happy once
happy twice
happy chicken soup
with rice.

8

MARCH

In March the wind
blows down the door
and spills my soup
upon the floor.
It laps it up
and roars for more.
Blowing once
blowing twice
blowing chicken soup
with rice.

APRIL

In April
I will go away
to far off Spain
or old Bombay
and dream about
hot soup all day.
Oh my oh once
oh my oh twice
oh my oh
chicken soup
with rice.

MAY

In May
I truly think it best
to be a robin
lightly dressed
concocting soup
inside my nest.
Mix it once
mix it twice
mix that chicken soup
with rice.

14

JUNE

In June
I saw a charming group
of roses all begin
to droop.
I pepped them up
with chicken soup!
Sprinkle once
sprinkle twice
sprinkle chicken soup
with rice.

JULY

In July
I'll take a peep
into the cool
and fishy deep
where chicken soup
is selling cheap.
Selling once
selling twice
selling chicken soup
with rice.

AUGUST

In August
it will be so hot
I will become
a cooking pot
cooking soup of course.
Why not?
Cooking once
cooking twice
cooking chicken soup
with rice.

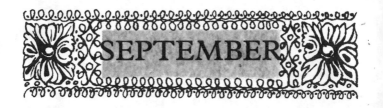

SEPTEMBER

In September
for a while
I will ride
a crocodile
down the
chicken soupy Nile.
Paddle once
paddle twice
paddle chicken soup
with rice.

OCTOBER

In October
I'll be host
to witches, goblins
and a ghost.
I'll serve them
chicken soup
on toast.
Whoopy once
whoopy twice
whoopy chicken soup
with rice.

NOVEMBER

In November's
gusty gale
I will flop
my flippy tail
and spout hot soup.
I'll be a whale!
Spouting once
spouting twice
spouting chicken soup
with rice.

DECEMBER

In December
I will be
a baubled bangled
Christmas tree
with soup bowls
draped all over me.
Merry once
merry twice
merry chicken soup
with rice.

I told you once
I told you twice
all seasons
of the year
are nice
for eating
chicken soup
with rice!